CELEBRATING THE FAMILY NAME OF WARREN

Celebrating the Family Name of Warren

Walter the Educator

Silent King Books
a WhichHead Entertainment Imprint

Copyright © 2024 by Walter the Educator

All rights reserved. No part of this book may be reproduced in any manner whatsoever without written permission except in the case of brief quotations embodied in critical articles and reviews.

First Printing, 2024

Disclaimer

This book is a literary work; the story is not about specific persons, locations, situations, and/or circumstances unless mentioned in a historical context. Any resemblance to real persons, locations, situations, and/or circumstances is coincidental. This book is for entertainment and informational purposes only. The author and publisher offer this information without warranties expressed or implied. No matter the grounds, neither the author nor the publisher will be accountable for any losses, injuries, or other damages caused by the reader's use of this book. The use of this book acknowledges an understanding and acceptance of this disclaimer.

Celebrating the Family Name of Warren is a memory book that belongs to the Celebrating Family Name Book Series by Walter the Educator. Collect them all and more books at WaltertheEducator.com

USE THE EXTRA SPACE TO DOCUMENT YOUR FAMILY MEMORIES THROUGHOUT THE YEARS

Celebrating the Family Name of Warren is a memory book that belongs to the Celebrating Family Name Book Series by Walter the Educator. Collect them all and more books at WaltertheEducator.com

USE THE EXTRA SPACE TO DOCUMENT YOUR FAMILY MEMORIES THROUGHOUT THE YEARS

WARREN

Deep in the earth where roots entwine,

Celebrating the Family Name of

Warren

The name of Warren claims its sign,

A lineage carved in soil and stone,

A legacy forever grown.

From ancient hills to river's bend,

The Warren name will never end.

With every dawn, with every flight,

Its spirit soars in morning light.

The Warren crest, both bold and true,

Like oak that thrives through wind and dew,

Stands tall against the tests of time,

Like oak that thrives through wind and dew,

Stands tall against the tests of time,

Its roots dug deep in every climb.

For every Warren knows their place,

A strength that hardship can't erase.

In hearths and hearts, the fire burns,

A strength that hardship can't erase.

In hearths and hearts, the fire burns,

A love for life with every turn.

Through winding paths and fields of green,

The Warrens walk, their footsteps seen,

Not seeking fame, but simple grace,

In every smile, in every face.

Celebrating the Family Name of

Warren

They plant their hopes, they sow their dreams,

In honest work, where sunlight gleams.

For family, strong as mountain's rise,

Is held in every Warren's eyes.

In days of old, when wars were fought,

The Warrens stood and never sought

To waver, bend, or flee the fight,

Their courage forged by honor's light.

Yet in their hearts, a gentler hand,

Could build and heal, could sow the land.

Through battle's storm or peaceful skies,

Their strength was found where wisdom lies.

Celebrating the Family Name of

Warren

Not just of earth, the Warren name

Is tied to dreams, to endless flame.

In starry night or silver stream,

It whispers of a greater dream.

For every Warren knows the call,

To stand with pride, to never fall.

Through trials fierce and moments small,

Celebrating the Family Name of

Warren

They rise again, they conquer all.

ABOUT THE CREATOR

Walter the Educator is one of the pseudonyms for Walter Anderson. Formally educated in Chemistry, Business, and Education, he is an educator, an author, a diverse entrepreneur, and he is the son of a disabled war veteran.
"Walter the Educator" shares his time between educating and creating. He holds interests and owns several creative projects that entertain, enlighten, enhance, and educate, hoping to inspire and motivate you. Follow, find new works, and stay up to date with Walter the Educator™

at WaltertheEducator.com

Milton Keynes UK
Ingram Content Group UK Ltd.
UKHW051141031124
450424UK00019B/1094

9 798330 497713